Achieving Financial Freedom

Learn how you can escape the rat race and stop trading time for money

Dr Harry Singh
BChD (Leeds), MFGDP (UK), GDC No: 72684

www.dentalpropertyclub.co.uk

All rights reserved. © Dr Harry Singh 2014

No part of this document may be reproduced, sold, stored in or introduced into a retrieval system, or transmitted, in any form or by any means (electronic, mechanical, photocopying, recording or otherwise), without the prior permission of the copyright owner.

Disclaimer: The author assumes no responsibility for the use or misuse of this product, or for any injury, damage and/or financial loss sustained to persons or property as a direct or indirect result of using this report. The author cannot guarantee your future results and/or success, as there are some unknown risks in business and on the Internet that we cannot foresee. The use of the information contained in this e-book should be based on your own due diligence, and you agree that the author is not liable for any success or failure of your business that is directly or indirectly related to the purchase and use of this information.

First printing: 2014

ISBN-13: 978-1495460234
ISBN-10: 1495460231

British Cataloguing Publication Data:
A catalogue record of this book is available from The British Library.

Acknowledgements

Without my wife, Sarb, this book would never have happened. She has given me undivided support and loyalty beyond my wildest dreams.

To my two children, Arjan and Rajneek, who make all the hard work worthwhile and never cease to make me laugh.

To all the coaches, mentors, authors and trainers I have learnt from in dentistry, property and personal development.

Contents

BIO 10

LIFE AFTER DENTISTRY 15

PATH TO FINANCIAL FREEDOM 27

GOALS – PLAN, DO AND IMPROVE YOUR LIFE PLAN 31

TIME – TAKING CONTROL OF YOUR DAY TO PRODUCE EXTRAORDINARY RESULTS 44

MINDSET – CONTROL YOUR MIND, DON'T LET YOUR MIND CONTROL YOU 57

THE PSYCHOLOGY OF MONEY – LEARN HOW TO WIN THE MONEY GAME 73

FINANCIAL FREEDOM FORMULA ALLOWS YOU TO NEVER WORK AGAIN … UNLESS YOU CHOOSE TO 87

WEALTH THROUGH PROPERTY 99

10 TIPS TO ESCAPE THE RAT RACE 112

CONCLUSION 117

Why Am I Writing This Book?

I and many of my professional dental colleagues shared the same frustrations of being a dentist and at times it seemed we were stuck in this rat race. I managed to escape the rat race and wanted to share my experience, my story, my strategies, my results so you can do the same.

In this book you will learn the following:

- discover wealth creation that does not require too much effort in the long term

- generate enough passive income to come out of dentistry completely (if you wish)

- how to keep it, grow it and protect it

- create wealth that is ethical and legitimate

- freedom to spend time as you wish with the people you love most, when and how you wish

- long term stability and growth

- reduce stress by working fewer hours and increasing quality family time

- maximise profits, be successful with investments and minimise risks

- don't overly expose yourself to too much risk or overstretch yourself

- generate income without having to work in the business

Did you know that there are three types of income – earned income, passive income and portfolio income? With passive income coming in every month, you can benefit in the following ways....less stress within your profession, more free time to develop your clinical and non clinical skills, extra revenue to improve your current practice or buy another practice......Just imagine what your life would feel like if you had all these benefits too.

- Discover – Why the wealthy invest in property and make money whilst they sleep.

- Learn – How you can buy 27 properties in 24 months.

- Action – To become financially free and only work when you want to

Using the principles I teach, I went from 0 to 27 properties in less than two years without using any of my own money. This property portfolio is worth over £7 million and produces a passive income of £8,000 a month, wherever I am in the world. I could have retired at the ripe old age of 35. There is nothing special about me, and you can do this too – by having access to these strategies and immersing yourself in the opportunity, which will lead to the results you desire.

About the Dental Property Club

The Dental Property Club was the brainchild of Dr Harry

Singh, a retired dentist. Whilst networking with my professional colleagues I realised many of them were not gaining maximum profits from their property investing, or they wanted to start in property but did not know how to begin. I have built a hugely successful and profitable property business and now wants to share my secrets with you.

The Dental Property Club can help you in two ways:

1. I offer workshops and mentoring programmes where I share my strategies which you can learn and implement in your property investing area

2. I am looking for financial joint venture partners: I use my time and experience to source property deals, you use your finances to fund the deal and then we can profit share together.

Bio

After I qualified from Leeds Dental School in 1996 I followed the traditional path of VT, Associate and then Principal. I have owned three dental practices.

I opened an award-winning private practice called aesthetics in Hertfordshire. We won many awards including – best marketing, best team, finalist for best facial aesthetics practice, and best aesthetics clinic. We ended up doing more facial aesthetics than dentistry. I loved every minute of it, and never regretted going into dentistry. It has provided me with so many opportunities.

During this time I started investing in property the traditional way (building up my deposit and then waiting before I had built up another deposit) and by chance stumbled upon the professional property secrets. In two years I had managed to buy and hold 27 properties and sell 6 properties. The profits from my property deals allowed me to buy into dental practices and set up two squat practices. The passive income paid for my financial commitments, so I was not overly stressed with the initial low cash flow from opening two squat practices.

This allowed me to free up my time from doing over 50 hours of clinical dentistry a week   and to spending quality time with my family and pursing my personal hobbies and interests.

I got to the stage where I was making more money from

property working only two days a week than I did working in dentistry full time, so I gave up dentistry in 2013 and reignited my passion for property. The portfolio is currently valued at around £7 million and gives me £8,000 passive income per month.

Harry's Dental Bio

1996 – Qualified from Leeds University as a General Dental Surgeon

1997 – Passed MFGDP(UK)

2000 – Joint owner of "Ninety Seven" dental clinic

2000 – Completed Certificate in Restorative Dentistry at Eastman Dental Institute

2002 – Owner of Vogue Dental Clinic

2002 – Trained in basic and advanced Botox, Dermal Fillers and Advanced Skin Health Restoration

2003 – 2006 – Vocational Trainer for newly qualified graduates

2007 – Trained in Advanced Skin Health Restoration including medical peels.

2007 – Opened aesthetics

2008 – aesthetics won Best Marketing at the Private Dentistry Awards

2008 – aesthetics won Best Team at Dentistry Awards

2009 – Finalist for Best Community Project at Private Dentistry Awards

2010 – Appointed on the editorial board of Premium Practice Dentistry magazine

2010 – Further advanced clinical masterclass training in Botox and Dermal Fillers

2011 – Wrote numerous articles on facial aesthetics for professional magazines

2011 – Mentor to the profession – asked to film for Vakmentor E-learning platform

2011-2013 – Advanced clinical training in advanced facial aesthetics and skin health restoration procedures

2012 – Speaker at the Dentistry Show at NEC on the business of setting up a facial aesthetics clinic

2012 – Asked to be on board of The Society of Aesthetics Practitioners (TSoAP) council

2012 – Speaker at the Odonti Dental Conference in Brighton on marketing techniques and tips on promoting your facial aesthetics clinic

2012 – Shortlisted from over 600 entries and a finalist in top 3 for best aesthetics clinic in My Face My Body awards

2012 – Voted in top 3 best facial aesthetics clinic in Private Dentistry Awards

2012 – Voted in top 25 aesthetic dentists in UK

2013 – Speaker at FACE conference on Referral Marketing Tips with your facial aesthetics business

Harry's Property Bio

2002 – Bought 1st property traditional way

2003 – 2007 – Mentored by property guru on the secrets of the professional property investor

2003 – Bought 1st property below market value and got all my money out on day 2

2005 – In 2 years held onto 27 properties, with no money left in any deal

2006 – Achieved financial freedom where I did not need to work at the age of 34

2007 – 2012 – Concentrated on dentistry/botox whilst receiving massive passive income every month from my property portfolio

2012 – Mentored a few close friends and family members regarding successful property investing

2013 – To date have spent over 10,000 hours learning about

property investing and networking with property professionals

2013 – Founder & CEO of Dental Property Club

2013 – 6 series article on wealth creation in Private Dentistry magazine

2014 – Speaking at Dentistry Live on wealth creation

Life after Dentistry

A number of my professional colleagues have asked me why I have given up dentistry and what I am doing now – and for me to let them in on the secret of what to do too! This is a frank and tongue-in-cheek look at why I will never drill or fill another hole, exploring the reasons behind what could seem an odd decision for such a young(ish) dentist, my insecurities, my fears and what drives me – and how I am now following my true passions in life.

'The greatest tragedy in life is to spend your whole life fishing, only to discover that it was not fish you were after.' Henry David Thoreau

We all have dreams and goals, things we love doing. However, life is filled with activities and commitments that have nothing to do with our dreams or goals. In both business and life we operate on auto pilot and live our lives in reactive mode. Sometimes we do what we think is right or what we think other people think will be right. I began to have this feeling a couple of years ago. At times it felt like I was a cross-eyed discus thrower; I would never set my own personal goals, but I would definitely keep everyone else entertained.

Design for life

I decided to take ownership of my life and my future, instead of letting life happen to me. If you don't design your own life plan, chances are that you will fall into someone else's plan. It was not as though I had failed; I had achieved success. I would have been more than comfortable if I carried on with what I was doing and where I was going. However, I wanted to be outstanding, more successful and make a difference.

Being successful is not an end goal: it is a journey, and those that are truly successful are the ones that know they will never reach the end of the journey, because becoming more day by day is the true definition of successful. I didn't want to slug my guts out for another 20 years doing something that was not my true passion and at the end of it, retire to 'enjoy' my life and receive a pension and say "Is that it?" I wanted my life back now. Success is the process of turning away from something to turn towards something better.

The Harajuku moment

I was visiting an elderly relative in hospital who did not have much more time left in this world. After chatting to them and walking back to my car, I reflected on my own life and had a Harajuku moment (an epiphany that turns nice-to-have/do into a must-have/do). I imagined myself as an old man rocking on my chair at the front of my house and reflecting on my time on this planet. Days are expensive: when you end a day, you have one less day to spend. Therefore I wanted to make sure I spent each one wisely. What I feared most was not having lived to the fullest extent possible, to come to the end of my life with my final words being, "I wish I had....." You listen to the older generation and I can promise you that 99% will not regret what they did, but what they didn't do. I want to prepare to die well, having no regrets. I quote from Buddha, 'Even death is not to be feared by those who have lived wisely.'

Back to the start

Let's start from the beginning; it's always a good place. From the age of 12 I have always wanted to be a dentist. I loved science; however, this was not the deciding principle. One day I went to the local library (for the younger generation, this was where we went to find out information in the days before we could 'google' anything we wanted to know), picked up a careers book and looked at who made the most money. The job title in the book said: **Dentist – aka licence to print money**. Not one to follow the crowd, I made sure no one in my family was a dentist and decided that this was the road to riches, fame, success and world domination.

I fluked my dental admissions interview by paying someone at my school to make a clay model to demonstrate to the panel my superb manual dexterity skills. I regurgitated with passion and enthusiasm that I would dedicate my life to caring for people, would give free dental care for the most needy, my goal being to rid the world of all dental disease, blah, blah, blah. (Mother Teresa would have enrolled me right then if she heard me.) Finally I graduated in 1996 from Leeds Dental School.

I followed the usual pathway of VT (God help me on what it is called these days) and associateship. As a typical Indian boy, I wanted to be the big boss, control everything, have the accolade of announcing that I was a business owner at wedding functions and hopefully this would allow me to marry a 'fit bird' – all arranged, of course.

To the max

After opening, buying and selling several dental practices, I was able to live a very good lifestyle, which included buying 'boys' toys' such as sports cars and watches, travelling the world and other pleasurable sins (which I cannot elaborate in case my wife reads this article). However, I decided that making money and all its trappings was fun, but the happiness was short lived. I felt like a drug junkie, and unless I injected myself regularly with the latest gadget or materialistic item, the happiness would not be sustainable. Contrary to popular misconception, the key to happiness is not having more (bigger houses, faster cars, more holidays). The key to happiness is **becoming** more.

Similar to many dentists who have spent several years drilling and filling under the NHS, I decided to improve and expand my dental menu of services. I was hoping that this would be the answer to the lack of appreciation and satisfaction I was getting from my chosen career. So I enrolled on as many courses as possible, which included, but was not limited to: smile makeovers, Invisalign, 6 month smiles, Inman aligner, ora lift, facial aesthetics, sedation, occlusion. With this vast experience, I wanted to work in a modern, contemporary dental practice which stood out from the run of the mill practices (it would be like wearing an Armani suit to work at McDonalds), so I set up a state-of-the-art private squat called aesthetics in 2007.

Dental dreams

This was my dream practice and it had everything I wanted. We won awards: best marketing – Private Dentistry Awards 2008; best team – Dentistry Awards 2007; shortlisted for a whole host of others, including best facial aesthetics practice – Private Dentistry Awards 2012, best aesthetics clinic – myfacemybody 2012, best drunk dentist – 2007, 2008, 2009, 2010, 2011, 2012....well, I made that one up, but if Carlsberg did awards...

I loved the creation of the aesthetics brand for our patients and my professional colleagues. I do not regret a minute of this journey and without aesthetics I would not have met or worked with some wonderful dental coaches, suppliers and colleagues.

However, as a business owner I was in at the deep end, each and every day. I could not let go and was not willing to delegate to others. Looking back at it now, it was stupid. It's like the owner of Liverpool FC playing every Saturday afternoon in the team on the pitch. The owner's job is to sit in the crowd and watch the game and then make the tough decisions. I had to be watching the game and not playing in it. I felt I could not do this with dentistry so, coupled with my true passions, I decided to sell the practice.

I made mistakes along the way, which I tend not to call mistakes but learning experiences. I don't dwell on them, as in life you can either have 'reasons' or 'results', or another way you can put it is you either have 'stories' or you have 'success'.

The meaning of life

There was something missing in my life; I was not living my ultimate mission in life. I had happiness, but did I really have meaning? Happiness is the moments of our life and meaning is the sense of connection. I felt disconnected, something like when a rotary file breaks away from the drill in the canal!

I had a very comfortable life. I am married with two children; I have a large family home, two cars, good holidays. I was thankful for my life. I knew I had made some tradeoffs – burning the midnight oil, less family time than desired, more weight than was ideal, not enough exercise, a bit more drinking than the recommendations (OK, a lot more drinking). However, I was in a similar position to my professional colleagues and we would regularly discuss these tradeoffs at dental conferences; it was an accepted part of the game we were in. But following my Harajuku moment, I asked myself the following questions:

1. Am I following my heart and being true to myself? What would my dream lifestyle look like? Not necessarily measured by what I had but by what I had achieved, had I changed people for the better?

2. Is my life focussed on the things that really matter to me?

3. Am I being the person I want to be in the world?

I researched the answers to these questions over the next few months, read many books, went to seminars, and listened to CDs in the car. I stumbled upon the answer and discovered that, like all strategies and procedures, it is very simple and easy to understand but difficult to practice. There are only two tasks in human life:

- to find ourselves (our destiny, to be true to oneself),
- to lose oneself (connect to something much larger, a greater significance).

In certain stages in our lives we know what the right thing to do is, but lack the courage to act.

Disclaimer: I am in no way implying that dentistry cannot change people's lives for the better or that as a profession we don't have a vital role to play in this world. I respect and am lucky to have friends who are amazing dentists, do a fantastic job and are following their life passions. I am just not one of those.

Follow your heart

On a slight tangent, whilst I was looking for these answers, I was working harder on myself than I was on my career. It seems fitting that I want to spare a few lines to some of the mentors that have had a significant impact on my personal development: Tony Robbins, Jim Rohn, Zig Zagler, Jack Canfield, Daren Hardy and Brian Tracy. You cannot do this all by yourself; as they say, your network is your net worth. You have to share your vision with your loved ones and my wife, Sarb has always been there for me and never doubted my decisions. I was going to follow my heart and my passion – and not my liver! – otherwise I would have ended up in a brewery for Jack Daniels. Oscar Wilde summed it up nicely: 'Be yourself, everyone else is already taken.'

Let's say you found out you only had six months to live. What are the five things you must do before these six months are up? Those five things you must do – are they not important enough to do regardless of how much time you have left?

Fight the fear

I believe that true power is to take action despite of fear. It was a brave move and my friends and family advised against it. They said I would be wasting all those years of studying; dentistry was a good reputable profession; what would the ladies in the Sikh temple think about me? They told me the grass was not always greener on the other side, and many dentists had returned to dentistry after failed alternative careers. If you know me well, then this was music to my ears (normally it's Bhangra music to my ears). I wanted to prove them wrong. But this was not the main driving force for me to change pathways: I wanted to do what I have always wanted to do but was afraid of the risk. We all have fear and F.E.A.R can either stand for Forget Everything And Run or Face Everything And Rise. So I decided to do the latter and rise in the way a small blue tablet takes hold of a certain men's body part.

Instead of playing the safe option of believing it when I saw it,

I knew that I would have to approach my next step along the lines of seeing it when I believe it. Now I didn't change careers without any experience with my new ventures. I once heard Lord Sugar say to go into any business, you must have passion, experience and knowledge about it; it really is as simple as this. Most people forget the knowledge and experience part and think passion alone will give them success. I disagree with the phrase "Do what you love and the money will follow". It's as absurd as me thinking, OK, eat what I love and my slim figure will follow. Choosing a business just for passion is fun; it is similar to making a baby, which is always more exciting than raising one. But without the correct knowledge and experience you won't be able to raise your child/business in the correct way. Don't go for the 'pin the tail on the donkey' approach to choosing your alternative career pathway.

It will take time and you will make mistakes.

Here and now

So what am I up to? I split my time between two business enterprises: I actively take part in both and get my hands dirty, and I also train others in what I do:

<u>1. Facial aesthetics</u>

I am a facial aesthetician – I love this aspect of my work. I have treated over 1,500 patients at aesthetics and I carry out these procedures weekly. I love the patient interaction with this type of work. There are no patients phoning me up in the middle of the night with a loose crown, broken tooth, sensitivity after a large restoration, pain after an incomplete endo! I love the fact that within 30 minutes you can boost their self esteem and confidence and they will forever be grateful.

2. Property

There are two strands to my property enterprise:

(a) Property investing – I have been investing in property for over 10 years alongside my dentistry career and I love this and am truly passionate about this business. I found it a perfect avenue to invest the money I made from dentistry and help me become financially free. I have amassed a portfolio worth over £7 million. I have enough passive income from this portfolio to never have to work again, but I very much enjoy this business.

(b) Dental Property Club – Whilst speaking to many dentists, I have heard many say that they are unsure where to invest their money. They are unhappy with leaving it in the bank and getting very poor returns and they want to get into property, but they don't know where to start. Using my own experience, I share my investment strategies regarding property investing, so they can avoid all the pitfalls and all the mistakes I have made.

I have succeeded in my new ventures because I have the basics of passion, experience and knowledge in my chosen fields and I follow the Ultimate Success formula of one of my mentors, Tony Robbins:

Target – have a clear focus on what you want to achieve

Act – if you don't act, your goals will just be dreams

Review – are the results you are producing taking you towards or away from your targets?

Flexible – you need to be able to adjust and adapt to keep on track

All you have to do is DECIDE – COMMIT – RESOLVE.

Free love

In summary, we have all heard people say, 'I love this so much, I would do it for free.' I have a different take on this, which is, 'I love this so much, it is the only thing I will do for money.' It can be done; it is not like 'Loch Ness Monster syndrome', where you have heard of it but never seen it. You have to take action NOW. You can spend your whole time planning your life, or you can live your life. I have never regretted choosing dentistry as a career; it has given me huge opportunities and the flexibility to pursue other avenues and follow my dreams.

'Twenty years from now you will be more disappointed by the things that you didn't do than by the ones you did do. So throw off the bowlines. Sail away from the safe harbor. Catch the trade winds in your sails. Explore. Dream. Discover.' Mark Twain

'We are always getting ready to live, but never living.' – Ralph

Waldo Emerson

Imagine you are nearing the end of your life and you're contemplating what your eulogy will say about you. Be honest with yourself: would you be happy to read what you have achieved, what you did... Could you have done more, given more, become more?

In life there are only two things that are important. No, it's not whether your crown taper was 6 degrees and your smile makeovers followed the Golden Proportion. The first is to find happiness (moments in our lives) and the second is to find meaning (a sense of connection).

Path to Financial Freedom

'You miss 100 per cent of the shots you never take.' Wayne Gretzy

Why wait for life to happen to you? Don't wait for the future – create and control the future....design the lifestyle of your dreams right now.

'We all have greatness within us.' – Les Brown

Learn how you can achieve financial freedom with multiple streams of massive, passive income.

Do you wish you had more time to relax and enjoy life?

Are you working all the hours available to you?

Do you not know where to invest your hard-earned cash?

Imagine being able to instantly gain all the knowledge you need to fast track your wealth, happiness and property profit right now.

Change starts with you. That's where my journey began. They say that formal education will make you a living, but self-education will make you a fortune. I spent more time, energy and money on my personal development than anything else. Once I mastered my goals, time management and mindset I looked at the strategies to obtain passive income and achieve financial freedom so I can choose when I want to work.

'Everyone thinks of changing the world, but no one thinks of changing himself.' – Leo Tolstoy

In this book you will have the opportunity to discover the ultimate strategies we all need to thrive and succeed. I will take you through the six step formula I personally use, so you too can achieve all the goals you want in life, achieve financial freedom by making more money, and work fewer hours – or you may never need to work again…unless you choose to.

This six step process is brought to you in the form of the following tools:

Goals – discover how to plan, do, review and improve your life plan

Time – take control of your day to produce extraordinary results

Mindset – control your mind and don't let your mind control you

Psychology of money – learn how to win the money game

Financial Freedom Formula – imagine never needing to work again….unless you choose to

Property – how to invest in this appreciating asset of the rich with a proven system to skyrocket your wealth

I recall these steps via the following acronym – GeT Moving in Property for Freedom and Profit. It is a simple process, but it will not be easy and without all the pieces of the jigsaw your results will be incomplete. Each step in this book will be like a treatment plan. It's important you follow the process in the correct order. If you carry out cosmetic dentistry before the periodontal condition is stabilised it will fail, and so will your probability of success.

It will take passion, dedication and energy, and if you commit to it you will be successful. If you succeed then the rewards will be *impact, influence* and *income* in your life and other people's lives.

'Do you want to succeed as bad as you want to breathe?' – Eric Thomas

'It is not for me to change you. The question is how can I be of service to you without diminishing your degree of freedom.' – Buckminster Fuller

Leave no regrets.

'The bitterest tears shed over graves are for the words left unsaid and deeds left undone.' – Harriet Beecher Stowe.

To leave this world with no regrets we must live with courage, moving towards what we want rather than away from what we fear. We can never guarantee success in our lives, but we can guarantee failure by deciding not to try at all. However, most of us – me included, initially – have such a great fear of failure or rejection that we die with our dreams, ideas, and aspirations inside us. Not now: we can decide our future.

> Now that you're out of my life
> I'm so much better
> You thought that I'd be weak without you
> But I'm stronger
> You thought that I'd be broke without you
> But I'm richer
> You thought that I'd be sad without you
> I laugh harder
> You thought I wouldn't grow without you
> Now I'm wiser
> Thought that I'd be helpless without you
> But I'm smarter
> You thought that I'd be stressed without you
> But I'm chillin'
> You thought I wouldn't sell without you
>
> Destiny's Child – Survivor

Please note that the information presented in this book is for educational purposes only and is not intended to be advice. If you are uncertain of any aspect of your finances you should seek advice from an independent financial advisor.

Goals - Plan, Do and Improve Your Life Plan

'Where there is no vision, the people perish.' – Proverb 29:18

How do you want to be remembered when you're not around anymore?

What contribution did you make to your loved ones and society?

Did you live, love and matter?

Did you leave a legacy?

If, as a dentist, you want to go from not achieving your goals to living your dream lifestyle, you will need to integrate the tools in this book.

Our lives are so complex today; we need a system of goal setting that delivers consistently. We must learn to create more choices in our lives and move ourselves in the direction we want, rather than react to the demands of the moment. It's easier to ride a horse in the direction it is going. You can learn anything you need to accomplish any goal you set for yourself. Every master was once a disaster. Compare yourself to where you are today as a dentist compared with your first day at dental school. If you were like me, you thought it would take forever and you might never achieve what your role models in dentistry have achieved.

'Don't have to see the whole staircase to take the first step.' – Martin Luther King

What are goals?

Success is goals and all else is commentary. Your life only begins to become great when you clearly identify what it is you want, make a plan to achieve it and then work on that plan every single day.

'Start with the end in mind.' – Stephen Covey

Why is it important to have goals?

I have a formula which is GS = GS, Goal Setting = Generates Success.

There was a famous study carried out in Harvard that showed that after ten years 13 percent of the class who had goals were earning, on average, twice as much as the 84 percent who had no goals at all. And the three percent who had clear, written goals were earning, on average, ten times as much as the other 97 percent put together.

An old story tells of a situation where an eagle egg accidentally rolls into a chicken's nest. As it hatches, it is treated as a chicken and brought up as a chicken and thinks it is a chicken. Then one day it sees the eagles soaring above and asks another chicken whether they could ever be like that. The other chicken tells him to stop dreaming; he'll always be a chicken. The moral of the story is that if you listen to the chickens around you, you will live and die like them, but inside we are all eagles.

How to do it

This process comes to you in the form of the 4 Ps – Plan – Perform – Probe – Progress.

1. Plan

Fail to plan and plan to fail. We need a life map and the best and easiest way is to use a 'wheel of life'. This exercise can be used for analysing both your personal or business life, or to map out a company. I will focus on the personal aspect. A typical wheel is divided into the following eight segments:

- Health and well-being

- Wealth

- Friends and family

- Playtime

- Relationships and romance

- Career/job

- Personal space/personal development

- Contribution/spirituality

Let's say you're starting off on a journey in the car. You have typed into your sat nav where you want to go. What's the first thing it works out? It's where you are right now, where you are starting from. So the wheel of life firstly lets you evaluate where you are right now in your life. Similar to our assessment and diagnostic tests such as radiographs, once we know the diagnosis, we can work out a treatment plan. If you don't know where you are now, how do you expect to know when you have reached your destination? It's like doing endodontics blindfolded. Actually, if you have seen my root canal therapies, then you probably would have thought I was blindfolded.

For each segment of the wheel of life have a line marked from 0 to 10. Mark on the line for each segment where you are now, with 0 being the lowest level of achievement/satisfaction and 10 being the highest level of achievement/satisfaction. This process is known as the Gap Map.

In addition to plotting these points in the wheel of life ask yourself the following questions regarding each segment:

- What have I achieved in the last year – successes, failures?
- What happened?
- How did it happen?
- What changes will I make?
- Key stresses?
- What did I celebrate?
- What did I enjoy?

Don't we do the exact same process in our dental audits and

peer reviews?

You can use these answers to help you be better prepared for attaining higher scores in each segment.

'Now the general who wins a battle makes many calculations in his temple before the battle is fought. The general who loses a battle makes a few calculations beforehand.' -The art of war – Sun Tzu

2. Perform

Now we know where we are and what got us here, the next stage is get more precise in each segment of the wheel of life. For each segment, focus on the following 10 points to give you the best chance of succeeding.

(i) Get clear – Clarity is power. Be as specific as possible. Your mind is a GPS = Goal Positioning System. Tell your internal GPS where you want it to go, and be as specific as possible. Your mind does not understand the goal of getting richer, but it will understand something specific, like wanting a passive income of £3,000 per month by this time next year. Decide exactly what you want in every life wheel segment – focus on what your ultimate vision is, what it is that is most important to you, and have a compelling reason why you want it. Be positive – if your aim is to lose weight don't frame it as "I don't want to be fat"; instead say, "I want to be lean and muscular".

What do you see in this…: Opportunityisnowhere

Opportunity is nowhere? Or opportunity is now here…

(ii) Get focussed – F.O.C.U.S = Follow One Course Until Successful. If you were a hunter chasing a deer, and you saw a rabbit cross your path, would you change direction and go after the rabbit? No, you would be focussed on your goal of hunting down the deer. Distraction is the enemy of success. It's like an implantologist being asked by a patient to carry out a small Class 1 cavity!

(iii) Get certain – What do you have to achieve and how can you do it? Write it down. List as many ideas as possible. Don't just think it, but INK it. What would you do if you knew you could not fail?

(iv) Get excited – Let the emotional juices flow. What would your ideal situation look like?

'Your vision is the promise of what you shall one day be.' – James Allen, As A Man Thinketh

Think like an athlete. They visualize themselves crossing the winning line first, or throwing the furthest, or jumping the highest. Take the bit between your teeth. There is nothing in a caterpillar that tells you it is going to be a butterfly.

(v) Get committed – Why is this goal a must? No one succeeded in dabbling. Be a completer. Sweat beats regret. Why is this goal a must, your compelling reason why. There is an old story where a General of an army was about to invade an island. The ship docked anchor and as the soldiers left the boat to invade the island, he burnt the boat. Now, there was no escape route for the soldiers, they would either succeed and capture the island, or they would die. Do you think the soldiers were more committed to win? How can you burn the boat and take the island?

The best 100m sprinters don't stop at the finish line, they carry on running right through it.

'If you spend an extra hour each day studying in your chosen field, you will be an national expert in that field in five years or less.' – Earl Nightingale

(vi) Get momentum – Do one thing now. What actions can you take within the next 24 hours to move towards your goal? P.U.S.H – Persist Until Something Happens.

(vii) Get wild – Set three targets for each goal – a minimum, your actual target, and an outrageous one. The minimum is what you can easily achieve, your target is what you expect to achieve and the outrageous one is the big fat hairy goal you have in your dreams. Make it SMART: specific, measurable, attainable, relevant (core values), timely. Remember the old sayings: You might as well be hanged for a sheep than a lamb. Aim for the moon and you might hit the stars; most people aim for the ceiling and hit the floor.

(viii) Get the best tools for success – mentors, proven map, skills, equipment. Your greatest asset is people, your mastermind group, the network around you. We all know birds of feather flock together, but make sure they are good birds (that's what I tell my wife when she sees me with an attractive woman). Stay away from negative people - some people are so negative that when they walk into a dark room, they start developing.

'If I have seen farther than others, it is because I was standing on the shoulders of giants.' – Sir Isaac Newton.

What are the potential obstacles to you achieving this goal?

(ix) Get aligned – Who do you need to become? Do your beliefs, values and goals align? To want more you have to become more. Success is not doing a process, but becoming the process. For example, when a car cruises at 70mph it runs more smoothly, requires less energy and power. Why? Because everything is aligned. Being misaligned is the same as a dentist trying to date a partner who does not brush their teeth or use floss and has severe halitosis.

(x) Get moving – As the Nike slogan says, 'Just do it'.

Goal Setting = Generates Success

3. Probe

You have to review your results, just like we regularly review the dental health of our patients. Are your actions and results taking you towards or away from your goals?

Like most people, I have failed in some of my goals and by probing and reflecting on what happened I have managed to change my results. I was getting stressed if things did not go according to plan, but then I started to focus my time and emotions on what I could control.

I found it hard to say no to people, especially when they used to offer me a quick cheeky JD and Coke; I would say "OK, let's make it a double!" By saying yes to everyone you are helping them achieve their goals but taking away from your own goals.

'I don't know the key to success, but the key to failure is trying to please everybody.' – Bill Cosby

'Those that cannot learn from history are doomed to repeat it.' – George Santayna

Feedback is the breakfast of champions and we must embrace it at all times.

'The reasonable man adapts himself to the world, the unreasonable one persists in trying to adapt the world to himself.' – George Bernard Shaw

Progress

It's not where you start, but where you are going. Life is like a marathon, with each runner having a different finish line. The real prize in a marathon is not to come in first place, but to run the race itself. It's a process of achievement, of reaching an objective and creating the potential to move on to an even greater goal.

Once we have reviewed our actions and results from our goals we can adapt and modify and improve and hence make progress in achieving our dream lifestyle.

Sloppy success is better than perfect theory. Just make a start, don't waste time waiting for the perfect time, it will never come. The phrase 'The proof is in the pudding' is the wrong way round. Visualise first and then take action. The past does not equal the future.

'The primary reason for failure is that people do not develop new plans to replace those plans that didn't work.' – Napoleon Hill

Mistakes

Why do we fail with goals? I have personally found there are three main reasons why we don't reach the goals we desire and ultimately have success.

Level of standards – You need to determine a level that is acceptable to you and raise your standards for yourself every day. Turn your 'shoulds' into 'musts'. I have banned myself from using words such as 'should', 'could', 'would' and donate £5 to charity if I or anyone else catches me saying any of these words.

Stories – You can either have 'stories' or 'success'; 'reasons' or 'results'. Drop the story and tell yourself the truth. Nothing gets better until you admit something is wrong. Understand the power of now. TNT – Today, Not Tomorrow.

Ineffective strategy – Success leaves clues. Get a mentor, someone who is doing what you want to achieve or is where you want to be. Develop a strategy that works; get the right tools.

Be prolific and not perfect.

Numbers

Studies (carried out by Smiles) show that the top 6% of the wealthiest people have written goals that they review daily and carry with them all the time.

According to the Massachusetts Department of Health, Education and Welfare, the most important risk factor in dying of your first heart attack is job satisfaction. Make sure you have a deeper meaning for your life than 'I'm on that rat race again!"

We all know about the compound effect, where small, smart choices + consistency + time = radical difference. From little acorns mighty oaks grow.

Take action within 24 hours, studies have shown that by taking a small step towards your goal within 24 hours of deciding on a particular goal, you will have a 80% more success rate.

Action to take now

If you want to get to the top, you must first get off your bottom. The only place success comes before work is in the dictionary. Don't watch how lips move but watch where the feet move – focus on what people are saying versus what they are doing. Do your wheel of life and know exactly where you are currently in your life. Then you will be able to:

- Stand up....for something, clear purpose

- Stand out.....innovate, differentiate

- Stand firm.....sustain your success

A burning desire is key to motivation, but it's determination and commitment that takes you to an unrelenting pursuit of your goal.

'Spectacular achievement is always preceded by spectacular preparation.' – Robert H Schulter

Goal Setting = Generates Success

Now we know what we want and how we are going to get there. The biggest reason people fail at achieving their goals is that they are poor time managers, they don't seem to have enough time. In the next chapter we will discuss how you can take control of your time.

You can also download my special report today for FREE: "10 Secrets To Successful Property Investing For Busy Dentists" at www.dentalpropertyclub.co.uk

Victor Frankl, a Nazi concentration camp survivor and author of 'Man's search for meaning', found his purpose in his future. He vowed that somehow he would survive, share his story and make sure that nothing like the Holocaust could ever happen again.

'Nothing can resist the human will that will stake even its existence on its stated purpose.' – Benjamin Disraeli

'Knowing is not enough, you must apply. Willing is not enough, you must do.' – Goethe

Time - Taking Control of Your Day to Produce Extraordinary Results

There are three ways to use your time – invest it, spend it and waste it. The difference between rich people and poor people is how they use time. Rich people spend money to save time and poor people spend time to save money. Which one are you? Once you have used your time up, you will never get it back; however, you can always find ways to make more money. For example, I don't do any housework or DIY around the house; I pay someone else to do it. It may cost me, let's say £100 per week, but the couple of hours I save, I use for creating passive income, and marketing/innovation for my business ventures, which leads to much higher income than the £100 per week I've spent.

If as a dentist you want to go from having not enough hours in the day to producing extraordinary results in less time then you need to integrate the tools here.

What's the first thing you did this morning? – Bet you it was reading messages or checking your mobile phone…why? Was it that important or critical? Then you must have checked some social media sites ..... then what's next, check your emails….is there something so important that you must do it right then? 80% of us sleep with a mobile phone next to us.

It is critical how you start each day because it sets the tone for the rest of the day. As dentists we have all had cases when the first patient in the morning is late or not very pleasant and it has an effect on us throughout the rest of the day. If someone else's agenda (emails, texts, status updates) is controlling your day, let them wait...focus on what's important to you. You should never wear a watch – when someone asks you what time it is, answer with "The time is NOW." The key is not to prioritise what's on your schedule but to schedule your priorities.

We live in a world where there are more demands placed on us and our time than at any other time in history. We have so many varied roles and duties to perform – parent, partner, dentist, employer, employee, friend, community champion, spiritual being and total athlete. How can we manage all these roles and still have time for ourselves?

We are all used to the 'to do' list and sometimes even when we complete it, we feel disappointed as we have not achieved the results we desire.

The result is the last action that happens when you undertake any activity. Before you get the results you want, there are two vital steps that you need to complete.

Purpose – What do you really want from this activity? What is your outcome? What is the specific result you're committed to achieving, e.g. Let's say you have set time aside to spend more time with your children, the actual purpose maybe to develop a deeper bond, or have a laugh, or improve their confidence.

Action – What specific actions must you take to make this happen?

What is time?

'It's being here now that's important. There's no past and there's no future. Time is a very misleading thing. All there is ever, is the now. We can gain experience from the past, but we can't relive it; and we can hope for the future, but we don't know if there is one.' – George Harrison

Time is often thought of as a river that flows in one direction and slows for no one, always sweeping everything and everyone along with it. We certainly experience the passing of time. We are born and live our lives feeling as though we are constantly being pushed and pulled by this unseen phenomenon.

Ask anyone on the street if they know what time is. They are sure to answer yes. But then ask them to explain it to you and they will almost certainly be at a loss for words.

I always go back to this when I feel I don't have enough time – schedule your priorities and do not prioritise what's on your schedule.

Many people get confused between effectiveness – closer to goal – and efficiency – doing anything the quickest way.

Time is nothing but a feeling. If you want more time, you simply need to manage your feelings. We have all had moments where time has flown by, e.g. participating in your favourite sport/hobby; you have no stress, and everything seems to flow effortlessly. And I bet you have also had moments when time stood still, when every second was an eternity, e.g. Filling out your CQC compliance paperwork. They're both extremes; time hasn't really sped up or slowed down. It isn't time that causes stress, it's the feelings we generate about the subject of time.

Instead of a 'to do' list let's change it to a results list. What are the results you want from any activity you need to do? The advantage of this is that you will be less stressed, you will do and achieve more and be more fulfilled.

Time Respect = Terrific Results

Why is this important to know?

Studies show that out of an average 45 hour work week, we have 17 hours that are unproductive. Imagine if you could double your results in the same time. If we don't control our time, it will control us and we will not produce the desired results. As Parkinson's Law states, a task will swell to the time it's been given. Maybe that's why my head swells when I get compliments constantly!

Time is a limited resource. Once it's gone, we cannot reclaim it back. We need to make better use of our time.

How to do it

This process comes to you in the form of the 3 Ds – Dump it, Delegate it, Do it. Before you decide what to do with anything, you must only touch it once. This means when you open something – a letter or email – make the decision right then which of the 3 Ds it falls into. Don't waste time saying you'll come back to it – most probably you won't, plus you will have wasted more time going back to it.

<u>Dump it</u>

If it does not serve you then bin it.

<u>Delegate it</u>

Delegating dramatically increases income. As a dentist I was the worst at delegating and I know many of my peers were the same. Why is this? Dan Sullivan says it's to do with being a 'rugged individualist' – which means when we started our businesses we did everything ourselves, invested time, money and energy and got good at whatever task we faced. We got used to this and just carried on with the flow.

There are many advantages of delegating:

- do more of what you love,

- do less of what you don't love,

- gain control of your life,

- have much more free time,

- tasks get done better, faster and easier,

- you have much more energy,

- your income goes up.

For example, when we refer to an endodontist it is because we don't have the passion to complete the treatment. Someone else can do it better and quicker, and it saves us time and stress to concentrate on stuff we enjoy doing.

(ii) How much should you delegate? – If you wish a task to be completed, do only those parts you enjoy and are great at, and delegate everything else. For example, at home with the task of dinner, my wife cooks it and I do the part I love – eating it.

(iii) Managing delegation – People respect what you inspect. Don't delegate via abdication, set clear instructions, review and improve.

If you don't have an assistant, you are one!

<u>3. Do it</u>

I always ask myself if the task is adding value and taking me towards my goals. If both answers are yes, then let's do it.

The system I use for managing my tasks is the RPM system devised by Tony Robbins.

RPM stands for Rapid Planning Management:

<u>Results focus</u> – What do I want? What's the result/outcome I am after? Not what should I do. Be very specific: clarity is more powerful; it takes more time but is worth it. Focus on outcomes more than activity. For example, if you have numerous to do lists, chunk them into eight wheel of life segments, and then if you only accomplish one of each you

still have a better balanced life. Where your focus goes energy flows. Don't be an activity manager but a results manager. Be productive and not active. Busy = broke, productivity = profitability.

<u>Purpose driven</u> – Do you have enough emotional juice to carry on and to overcome any obstacles? Why, and what is your purpose?

<u>Massive Action Plan</u> = MAP, for real and lasting results.

Implementing a system like this will take longer initially, like writing your full name with the opposite hand, but over time it will become faster.

In property we can use the power of leverage, where the bank will help you fund part of the purchase and you profit from 100% of the increase in price. So we can also use leverage to save ourselves time and get our results much more quickly. How many hours do you think Bill Gates has in a day? If you said 24, you would be wrong. He has on average 94,000 employees, so he has 94,000 x 24 = 2,256,000 hours per day to use. There are many different types of leverages available to every one of us:

OPT – other people's time

OPM – other people's money

OPC – other people's contacts

OPS – other people's systems

Law of leverage:

$$10+10+10+10+10=50$$

$$10 \times 10 \times 10 \times 10 \times 10 = 100,000$$

The only difference is the angle of the two lines between the numbers.

We all know the traditional sayings "Early to bed, early to rise" and "The early bird catches the worm". For example, when I attended my first property auction, I decided to leave home early and I arrived 60 minutes before the auction began. There was only me and an older gentleman there. We started chatting and to cut a long story short, I found out he was a property tycoon who had over 100 properties. Due to the relationship we had built pre the event he could see I was very passionate about this field, and he agreed to mentor me. I started to use his strategies to build my own property portfolio and brought 27 houses in 24 months.

I am often asked how people can relate this to business. You can use the RPM system for your dental business and for your team. With regards to business I have an additional tool to help me maximise my time.

- Projects – 3 maximum projects, and list the 5 things you must do in each to move it forward

- People – List the people you need to reach out to and the people you are waiting for

- Priorities – 3 main things you must complete today, no matter what

Time Respect = Terrific Results

Numbers

On average you have 25,000 mornings in your lifetime – don't waste them. 25,000 times you get to open your eyes, face the day, and decide what to do next. I don't know about you, but I have had a lot of those mornings slip by – especially if there was a dental awards event the night before and I met my friend Jack Daniels!

Manage your energy and not your time. Work out when you are the most productive and schedule your big rocks/must dos then. I used to do the same in dentistry; I would have my big cases, such as smile makeovers and quadrant dentistry, in the mornings and then in the afternoon my examinations, simple restorations, etc.

Five master steps of planning your time

Capture – ideas, wants, needs

Create – RPM plan

Commit – block time and resolve your musts

Schedule it – imagine and anticipate the results and rewards

Complete, measure and celebrate the results

Time Respect = Terrific Results

Mistakes

1. Addiction to distraction – An average person wastes two hours per day. We as a society spend 100,000,000 minutes per day playing Angry Birds. My solution for avoiding distraction was to write down everything that used to distract me. When you use this, you'll be shocked at how much time you are wasting. For example, I found myself looking at my email inbox every five minutes, so now I only open emails twice a day: once at midday and again at 6pm. Obviously if you are at front of desk on reception and receiving email enquiries from patients, then you will be checking them regularly.

2. Procrastination – At work when I had an important task to complete, firstly I would start to use the paper shredder or tidy up the office. I had a tidy desk but the task would take forever to complete. There are two types of people: the first is the optimistic procrastinator, who thinks they have all the time in the world and can leave the main task to the end. The second is the pessimistic procrastinator, who stresses that they will never have time to complete the task, no matter what. Which one are you?................Can't decide? Procrastination is not an illness (unlike smoking or over eating); it is that you are attempting to do something you don't feel passionate about. Procrastination is the effect and not the cure; you cannot cure an effect. The simple solution, as mentioned previously, is to delegate.

3. Multi tasking - Learn to separate the major from the minor. A lot of people don't do well, simply because they major in minor things. Focus on one thing: you can't get a baby in a month by getting nine women pregnant!

Most of us have read Tim Ferris's book The 4 Hour Work Week. I disagree with the title. If you ask anyone who is successful (Richard Branson, Lord Sugar) none of them only work 4 hours per week. The only way a four hour week is meaningful and progress, is if you are a couch potato and you have been doing zero hours per week on useful activities, then yes, you are making progress by increasing this to 4 hours per week!

Schedule thinking time. This is the most underestimated use of our time. The brain/mind consists of white space and we need to use this to our advantage. For example, have you ever had trouble recalling someone's name (or even called the patient the wrong name) and then stopped thinking about it, carried out another task and all of a sudden the name pops into your head? That's the magic of thinking time. When I am on the train or in the shower, I come up with some amazing ideas – well, I think they are amazing, so I always have a notepad or dictaphone on hand to record these moments of inspiration.

Time Respect = Terrific Results

Tips

I agree with the automation Tim Ferris describes and this is where technology can help you instead of ruling you. In dentistry we can use technology to our advantage, such as computerised records and digital radiographs. I love automation; it's like property investing – work once and get paid forever. I use the "set and forget" principle.

Some of the time saving apps I use are:

- Data storage – Dropbox, Google Drive
- Communication – Skype, GoToMeeting, Google Hangouts, join.me, groupme (group text)
- Organisation – invoice2go, Instapaper, business card scanner, voice memos, Evernote (notes), 30/30

Summary

Stress in life comes from making things more important than they really are. Failure in life comes from making things less important than they really are. In closing:

– Act on the important – don't react to the urgent

– Go for the extraordinary – don't settle for the ordinary

– Schedule the big rocks

– Rule your technology – don't let it rule you

– Fuel your fire – don't burn out, maintain high vitality

Time Respect = Terrific Results

We know what goals we are aiming for and we know how to maximise our time to get the results we want. However, if you don't get this next part mastered, you will be doomed to fail. This critical element is learning to control your mind, and we will cover it in the next chapter.

In John Izzo's book, '5 secrets you must do before you die' he outlines the following five things – will you do these before time runs out on you?

- Be true to yourself
- Leave no regrets
- Become love
- Live the moment
- Give more than you take

Time Respect = Terrific Results

Mindset - Control Your Mind, Don't Let Your Mind Control You

Success is simply a matter of luck. Ask any failure.

'I count him brave who overcomes his desires, than him who conquers his enemies, for the hardest victory is the victory over self.' – Aristotle.

From the previous two chapters we know the goals we will be aiming for and how to maximise our time to get the results we want. But if you don't master this next tool you will be doomed for failure. This critical element is learning to control your mind.

Let's say you wanted to start investing in property. You may ask yourself what it takes to become a successful property investor. Most people expect some kind of quick formula that will help them to become successful overnight and they can't wait to chew on the bone. As with anything, knowledge is essential, but knowledge has limitations without the right mindset. We can manage and control our lives if we know how our mind works, why we make certain decisions and how to master our mind.

If as a dentist you want to go from your mind mastering you to mastering your mind you need to understand why you make certain decisions and what the consequences of those decisions are.

Would you be interested in learning to control your mind so

you will always make the right choice for you in any given situation?

Thinking does not happen to you; it's something you do. For example, if you want to try to be sad, you first have to think sad thoughts; you can't just get the result of sadness immediately. As an avid Liverpool football fan I have become a master of being sad, especially with all my wife's family supporting Manchester United.

A turtle only makes progress when it sticks its head out.

Your mindset is everything when it comes to successful property investing. The combination of the right knowledge and right attitude is unbeatable. For example, in 1954 Roger Bannister was the first person in history to run a mile within four minutes. Before this great achievement it was thought impossible to do this. Yet less than 12 months after Roger Bannister's record, other runners achieved the same feat. So what changed? It wasn't a new diet, running shoes or technique. They had just changed their attitude and belief system.

If you can't believe you will locate bargain properties at 25% below their market value, then these deals will not present themselves to you. And without the right attitude you will miss these great opportunities. When I first started in property, I thought that people would not sell their house for thousands of pounds less than the open market value. I had to overcome this mindset obstacle and once I did, as if by magic I started seeing and converting great deals.

I always remember the T.E.A.R formula when it comes to getting the right mindset. Everything starts with Thoughts. This sparks off certain Emotions, which lead us into Action, which eventually determines our Results. We can see that our initial thoughts determine the results we achieve in life. That is why it is so critical to have the correct mindset and frame of mind, otherwise all the skills and knowledge in the world will not achieve the results you desire.

Another way to look at it is to say we live in two worlds: our inner world and our outer world. The inner world controls the outer world. Whatever attitudes, beliefs, thoughts we have will follow us in our outer world through the actions we do and the actions we don't do, and this will produce the results we get. I have spent more time and money developing myself and learning about mind power than I have on strategies, skills and knowledge. 80% of everything we do is psychology and 20% is mechanics.

Success is in your DNA.

What are your limiting beliefs? Answer the following questions and you will discover them.

– When under pressure, you …

– You often feel guilty about …

– You are afraid of …

– You always try to …

– When the unexpected happens, you …

What you measure improves. Once you have found your answers, provide alternative solutions. For example, for me, 'When under pressure I panic' translated into 'When under pressure I think about the situation calmly and ask for support'.

I have purposely spent more time in this chapter explaining how the mind can control us, as I have on mastering your mind process. The why is more important than the now. Let's now look at the practical steps you can take to retake control of your thoughts and, ultimately, your results.

What has your mindset got to do with your results?

There are two things that determine your success in life:

How you communicate with yourself within your own mind – internal communication

How you communicate with others – external communication

Before I understood this, I used to spend the most time, money and energy learning the skills to communicate with my patients, but I was concentrating on the wrong communication. I needed to look at my internal communication (little voice, my inner dialogue) – the communication I had with myself. If you don't think you have an inner voice, then that was it, the one that just said "I don't exist". Life is 10% what happens to you and 90% how you respond to it. What you sow, so you shall reap.

Your income can grow only to the extent you do – your income zone is directly related to your comfort zone. Your net worth won't exceed your self worth.

You can have two people sitting next to each other in a dental course, let's say on marketing. They both listen to the same content, strategies and opportunities. A year later, one has not applied anything into practice, and he/she is in the same place as a year ago, whilst the other dentist has used the tools and strategies and sky rocketed to success with their dental business...Why?

'The bigger the why, the easier the how.' – Jim Rohn.

Why-Power is greater than Will-Power.

People think success is a straight line progressing upwards, but is it really a zig zag of success, obstacles and failures. Unless you have a strong WHY you're likely to give up at the first obstacle.

'There are more things in heaven and earth than are dreamed of by mere mortal man.' – Shakespeare

Nothing happens by chance. The quality of our lives is brought about by the quality of your thinking. Everything affects everything else. Wherever we go, whatever we do, our thoughts are creating our reality.

'So think as if your every thought were to be etched in fore upon the sky for all and everything to see, for so, in truth, it is.' – Book of Mirdad

You are living simultaneously in two worlds, two realities: the inner reality of your thoughts, emotions and attitudes and the outer reality of people, places, things and events. We need to separate the inner and outer worlds. However, what most people do is become dominated by the outer world, and use the inner world as a 'mirror' for whatever happens to them; they are in reactive mode. This inner world is a powerful force whose influence is felt in every aspect of your life. It is, in fact, the major and most important part of who you are, and it's the main cause of your success or failure. Imagine for a moment that for every thought we either gained a pound or lost a pound, depending on the type of thought. We would pay more attention to our inner world if we used this accounting system...but this happens every day of your life.

Self concept

Your self concept drives everything. I mentioned before I use the T.E.A.R. Formula to break down how our mind controls our results in life. Thoughts lead to Emotions giving you certain Actions, which lead to the Results you have. For example, I have a constant battle with my weight. On certain days my thoughts are that I hate my body shape and that gives me negative emotions which drive me to take action, whether this is to exercise more or to go on a diet, and this results in me losing weight. On other days I am not thinking about my weight, so I don't have any strong emotions attached to my body shape, therefore I take no action to change my body shape, hence I am more likely to over eat and drink, resulting in weight gain. I know what the problem and solution is (consume fewer calories than you use) but it is 'why' I want to do it that leads to action and results. In life 80% is why (psychology) and 20% is how (mechanics).

In James Allen book 'As A Man Thinketh', he states a man can only rise, conquer and achieve by lifting up his thoughts. Master your mind.

We can see how important our self concept is, but where does it come from? It is made up of three parts –

(i) Self ideals – characteristics you want to have that you observe in others that you consider as role models or are emotionally connected to. If you see a trait in others, then you have that same trait, like it or not – otherwise you would have not seen it.

Self image – what do we see about ourselves in the mirror?

(iii) Self esteem – how you feel about yourself – do you like yourself? My wife tells me I have mastered this skill a bit too much. Low self esteem leads to doing things you know you should not do, e.g. eating chocolate when on a diet.

Business and life is a game of influence. To influence anyone, you have to know what influences you as well as them. There are two forces that influence our decisions.

The first is our state, moment to moment. If you're in a fearless state, you will make conservative decisions; if you're happy, you'll make more outrageous decisions. For example, recently after a few drinks I was talking to my mates and we all volunteered for a parachute jump. In the cold light of day, it was not the best decision to have made.

The second is our blueprint (which I will discuss in relation to money in the next chapter), how our beliefs and our view of the world dictate how we see things.

Before you even consider property investing you need to believe in yourself, as without self belief you will join the majority that have tried, but failed. I have heard many reasons why dentists think they can't make money from property, such as:

- I don't have the time
- I don't have the contacts
- I don't have the experience
- I am not good looking enough
- I can't give up dentistry
- I'm the wrong colour
- I'm the wrong sex
- I'm too short (that's for the Gujarati dentists!)

Do you have any of these limiting beliefs preventing you from achieving the success you deserve? What is your self concept of your property income? Do you honestly believe you can … buy 27 properties in 24 months … have £8,000 passive income per month ... have a property portfolio worth over £7 million...? If not, guess what will happen ... you will be proved right because you won't achieve these goals.

'If you think you can or cannot, you're right.' – Henry Ford

'Whatever the mind of man can conceive and believe he can achieve.' – Napoleon Hill.

Success is in your DNA.

Steps to control your inner world

Become aware of it – The mind is like a garden which can be cultivated or neglected and you are the master gardener. You will reap the harvest of your work or your neglect.

Visualisations – This is using your imagination to see yourself in a situation that hasn't yet happened – picturing yourself having or doing the thing you want, and successfully achieving the results you desire. Follow these steps to successful visualisation: decide what you want in the positive – relax for 5 minutes – spend 5-10 minutes visualising the reality you want – any thought put into your mind, and nourished regularly, will produce results in your life.

Seeding – *'When an object or purpose is clearly held in thought, its precipitation, in tangible and visible form, is merely a question of time. The vision always precedes the realisation'* – Lillian Whiting.

If visualisation is creating scenes or pictures in your own movie, then seeding is like adding the sound track, only instead of words you are adding the feelings that accompany the pictures. Imagine what it would feel like after achieving the goal in your visualisation exercise.

Affirmations – These are simple statements repeated to yourself silently or aloud. You can do them anywhere: in the car, when walking, etc. Keep them in the positive and short – every day in every way I am getting better and better, that kind of thing.

Acknowledging – Nothing succeeds like success. We are all guilty of spotting our own failures and mistakes very easily and quickly. Where we focus on, our energy flows. Therefore isn't it a better use of our time and energy to focus on our victories? Stop reading and write down at least 20 good points about your life, past or present. Your list can include such things as: I dress well, I am good at my job, people like me, I work hard, etc.

Everything is selling, but the biggest sale is the sale we make to our little voice. What does yours sound like when you argue with yourself over a good idea, e.g. going to the gym?

Believe me when I say that psychology and attitude are paramount to your success, and probably more important than all the tips, steps and 'secrets' [there are no secrets!] that you are getting here. Once you have the right mindset, you will ALWAYS find the 'how to.'

Ultimately, everything we do in our lives is driven either by our need to avoid pain or our desire to gain pleasure. You are either a puller (away from pain) or a pusher (towards pleasure). However, we will do far more to avoid pain than we will to gain pleasure.

We make our decisions, which leads to our results in life, according to what stops us. Whenever you put off something, it's because it's more painful to do something than take no action.

How to do it

This process comes to you in the form of the 3 Rs – Ritual, Restraining your little voice, Reflection.

1. Ritual – I call this my hour of power. Every morning straight after I have woken up and before I do anything, I will carry out the following:

- Physiology – emotion is created by motion, so I will I get myself in an empowering/peak state by either going for a jog or brisk walk, or doing star jumps.

- Focus and beliefs – whatever you focus on, energy flows. So I write down what I am grateful for, starting with myself, then the segments of the wheel of life. Then I visualise what I want in life as if I have already achieved it and lastly I focus on what I want to create today.

- power of language – I use affirmations to repeat certain phrases with enough emotional intensity that I start to believe it. For example I say, 'Handsome

Harry is a hunk' ... only joking, what I really say is, 'Every day and in every way I am improving.'

Now you may be laughing at this point and thinking I am crazy. Well, I would rather people think I am crazy and successful than think I am normal and mediocre. Trust me, once you repeat this process, amazing things will happen. I recommend you do this for at least 10 days – the 10 day challenge – and if you don't notice a difference then stop, but I bet you won't once you see the results. Master your mind.

2. Restraining your little voice. You can't silence it but you can control it and manage it (like a husband or wife) to your advantage. Here are the ways I master it:

- Acknowledge you have one or several little voices. Mine used to speak when I was presenting a high value treatment plan and my little voice would knock off a grand before I opened my mouth.

- Step outside of it and look at it objectively.

- Ask yourself where it came from – beliefs, past experiences etc.

- Reprogramme it.

Don't let emotions run high. When emotions are high, intelligence is low.

If you don't want to think certain things, then don't say them. Blame = be lame.

3. Reflection

– What have been your limiting beliefs?

– What has your limiting beliefs cost you?

– How has your mind controlled you?

– What changes will you make happen now?

Mistakes

– No thought lives in your head rent free. I used to have some negative thoughts about certain situations or people and thought they would not affect my results or actions. Boy, was I wrong. It's like you living in a block of flats: there are six levels and on all levels apart from one are law abiding citizens, but one floor is full of criminals, drug addicts, alcoholics. What do you think will happen to the entire block of flats after six months? Correct: it will be full of criminals, drug addicts and alcoholics. It's like when a group of dentists get together; it just takes someone to moan about the NHS contract, CQC, patients and then we all start.

– Not letting go. It's known as sunken costs. We are irrationally attached to time, energy and money we've invested in the past. It's already gone, so should not figure into our judgements, but it does. Don't cry over spilt milk, but it's perfectly ok to cry over spilt (insert your favourite alcoholic beverage).

– Not going out to play to win. How you do anything is how

you do everything. I used to play small when I thought it did not matter. This is perfectly illustrated with the England football team currently. If you are going to be in the major finals of a tournament you would only go if you thought you were going to win. Otherwise what is the point? Now the press and FA are indicating we are not good enough and so should use it as a learning experience. I am all for learning, but this is ridiculous. They have already told themselves they won't win and by now you will know what thoughts lead to ...yes, their results.

Master your mind.

Tips

I spend more time, money and energy on personal development than any other aspect in my life: more than on facial aesthetics, more than on dentistry, more than on property investing, more than on time with family and friends and even eating. Why? Because I understand that skills pay the bills, that the more you learn the more you earn, that formal education will make you a living and self education will make you a fortune.

'Nothing can stop the man with the right mental attitude from achieving his goals, nothing on earth can help the man with the wrong mental attitude.' – Thomas Jefferson.

Action plan

Here are some actions you can take immediately to feed your

mind useful material so you can achieve the results you desire.

– Physical obesity is not caused by the overload of available food, it is caused by the over consumption of low quality food. The same is true for mental obesity. It is not the overload of available information, it is the over consumption of low quality information. The solution is to go on a diet for both – a food and information diet. Avoid useless information such as news, press, gossip, forums, then give yourself several servings of mind-healthy, nutrient-rich information every day.

– In Ellen Langer's book, 'Mindfulness' – in life and business we operate on autopilot and live life in a reaction mode. Focus on what is going on around you. Transform problems into opportunities. See things differently, notice what you normally don't notice, change old meaning into new meaning, notice what you're missing.

To change your life, you must change your neuro associations. This can be achieved in three steps:

Get leverage on yourself – something must change, I must change, I can change.

Interrupt your current pattern of association – make a radical change in what you say or how you move your body.

Condition a new empowering association – install a new choice and reinforce it until it is conditioned. Ultimately this will become a habit.

Summary

You are here today where the thoughts of yesterday have brought you and you will be tomorrow where the thoughts of today take you. Who is the only person reading this book right now that can control what you do and achieve in the future.....? It's you!

'We are what we repeatedly do, excellence therefore is not an act but a habit.' – Aristotle

You have to do it yourself (you can't take a horse to water), and you can't do it alone (get your teeth into that one until it sinks in).

We have now covered the three basic but essential strategies to leading a successful and prosperous life. Next we'll look at the financial aspect of how to make you feel prosperous. In the next chapter I shall look at what you have been taught or believe about money will directly affect how much of it you make.

You can also download my special report today for FREE "10 Secrets To Successful Property Investing For Busy Dentists" at www.dentalpropertyclub.co.uk

'Small minds discuss people, average minds discuss events, great minds discuss ideas'. – Eleanor Roosevelt

Master your mind.

The Psychology of Money - Learn How to Win the Money Game

'Money won't make you happy, but it will help you enjoy your misery in a lot of interesting places.' – Walter Hailey.

We have now covered the three basic but essential strategies to lead you to a successful and prosperous life. Let's look at the financial aspect now – how to make you feel prosperous. In this chapter I shall look at what you have been taught or believe about money and how it will directly affect the amount you make.

Are you working too hard with little to show for it?

Do you consider yourself a fairly high achiever but you are not achieving your financial potential?

Are you afraid you won't be able to retire when you plan to, or have the lifestyle you dreamed of?

If you answered yes to any or even all of these questions I have the solutions for you. If you want to discover the secrets of the rich then please read on

Winning the money game

Before we look at money and your beliefs let's think about what money is to you and its importance in your life.

If as a dentist you want to go from never having enough money to living with abundance you will need to understand your beliefs about money.

What is money and how important is it?

What does money mean to you?

Money is simply a means of exchange. Previously when we lived in the barter system, money was created to represent the value of those goods and help people exchange goods and services more easily. Money is nothing but the measure of the value that you create and deliver for people. The more value you create for people the more money will be attracted to you, therefore money flows to the people who are providing the most amount of value.

For example, many of my dental patients valued more the results they had from Botox therapies and what it gave them compared to maintaining optimal periodontal health. They could always find the money and would never cancel a Botox appointment but the same patient would quite easily cancel and not value a 30-minute appointment with the hygienist. In essence, we must understand what the patient values and will be willing to pay for.

If you want more money, you don't start off with, 'How can I make more money?' Instead ask yourself, 'How can I create more value?' You create value by solving problems for people and giving them what they want. Dentistry is solving problems of bad dental health; all business is solving one kind of problem or another that customers are willing to pay for.

Money is one of the most emotionally charged issues of our

lives. Some of us are even willing to give up things that are much more valuable than money in order to get more of it. Money by itself is neither good nor bad – it's neutral. Money is merely a medium of exchange. It allows us to simplify the process of creating, transferring and sharing value within a society, so saving us the inconvenience of bartering. We don't want more of this piece of paper with the queen's head on it; we want more of what this piece of paper can provide us.

Money is not everything, but it is up there with oxygen. No amount of money will ever make you wealthy. The secret to wealth is gratitude. If you think that money is the answer to all your life problems, then your problems will never go away. Money is not the answer. As rap star The Notorious B.I.G. said, "Mo money, mo problems." Money is not everything; in fact, in my personal list it is number four, behind family, health and friends.

Most people seem to have made settlements with life – settling for less than what they really believe they can have, whether it be unfulfilling relationships, or jobs that they hate going to. People constantly struggle for money or feel that happiness is only for the lucky few. These are certainly some of the feelings I have experienced. What about you? What settlements have you made? What are you tolerating in your life? My question to you is what are you putting up with it? You know you deserve better, don't you?

Why is it important to learn about money?

Do you have to be good at maths? Not necessarily. There are

three kinds of people: those that can count and those that can't!

Money and financial problems are the second most cited reason for divorce. Do you know what the first is? It's marriage!

Rich people believe the primary reason to work is to earn money to invest and create passive income structures so they can win the money game and become financially free.

As I mentioned in the previous chapter, the 'why' is more important than the 'how'. So write down now why you want to be wealthy and create passive income. You will have your own reasons, and they may be the same as mine or not, but here are mine:

- Support my family and future generations

- To do what I love and impact on as many people as possible to enrich their lives and get handsomely rewarded at the same time

- Best way to help the poor is not to become poor yourself

- Teach my children the value of money, because no one else will

Winning the money game.

Money beliefs

As I mentioned in chapter three, our beliefs and thoughts lead to our emotions, actions and ultimately our results in life – the T.E.A.R formula. Why do so many people fail to achieve financial abundance in a world where economic opportunities surround us? There is enough for everyone, just like the oxygen we breathe. No one complains that someone is taking your oxygen away; there is an abundance of it available, just like money.

What are your attitudes to wealthy people? Do you feel admiration or jealously, anger, resentment? Holding on to anger and resentment is like drinking poison and expecting someone else to die.

What were you taught about money when growing up? Money does not grow on trees, you have to work hard to make money, rich people rob the poor?

Money and happiness is completely unrelated. Some of the happiest people are the poorest and some of the most miserable people are wealthy beyond imagination.

Now you may be thinking that having lots of money is bad and we should not aspire to this mentality. I recently spoke to a university professor at a dental school about wealth creation and property investing. He agreed with the principles and could see how it made sense. However, he did not want to get involved. His reason? Because "I am an academic. We are not supposed to be interested in wealth creation."

My parents used to say things like rich people were greedy and that to become rich you would need to hurt others. If your motivation for acquiring money or success comes from a non-supportive root such as fear, anger, or the need to "prove" yourself, your money will never bring you happiness.

Here is a list of different beliefs that rich and poor people have regarding money, borrowed from T Harv Eker's book, "The Millionaire Mind".

1. Rich people believe I create my life, poor people believe life happens to me.

2. Rich people play the money game to win, poor people play the money game not to lose.

3. Rich people are committed to being rich, poor people want to be rich.

4. Rich people think big, poor people think small.

5. Rich people focus on opportunities, poor people focus on obstacles.

6. Rich people admire other rich and successful people, poor people resent rich and successful people.

7. Rich people associate with rich/successful people, poor people associate with negative/unsuccessful people.

8. Rich people are willing to promote themselves and their value, poor people think negatively about selling and promotion.

9. Rich people are bigger than their problems, poor people are smaller than their problems.

10. Rich people are excellent receivers, poor people are poor receivers.

11. Rich people choose to get paid on results, poor people choose to get paid based on time.

12. Rich people think 'both', poor people think 'either/or'.

13. Rich people focus on their net worth, poor people focus on their working income.

14. Rich people manage their money well, poor people mismanage their money well.

15. Rich people have their money work hard for them, poor people work hard for their money.

16. Rich people act in spite of fear, poor people let fear stop them.

17. Rich people are constantly learning and growing, poor people think they already know.

How

The process to win the money game comes to you in the form of five steps that I have labelled M.U.S.I.C.

<u>M – Money management</u> – I personally use this system to allocate the income I generate from various activities. Before I

spend a single penny my monthly income is divided into the following pots.

– 55% – essential jar to pay household expenses

– 10% – personal development courses, mentoring and products

– 10% – savings pot for bigger purchases such as holidays

– 10% – financial freedom account – passive streams of income, e.g. property

– 10% – fun jar – on things I enjoy, no limits on this one

– 5% – community and charitable donations

U – Understand debt – good debt versus bad debt. Good debt is an investment that will grow in value or generate long-term income, e.g. property. Bad debt is debt incurred to purchase things that quickly lose their value and do not generate long-term income, e.g. cars.

S – Simplify – stop spending everything you make. Small sacrifices made today will compound into magnificent opportunities in the future. Don't buy that luxury car or rent a luxury penthouse. Save your money and invest in a property where rental profits can pay for the car lease or the luxury penthouse rent, so you use other people's money and you're sitting on an appreciating asset.

I – Instant gratification – this is a killer and is the number one reason why most people do not achieve the wealth they want.

As with all things it's what happens in your mind and the thoughts you have regarding delaying any purchases. Stop buying things on impulse. When we buy things, we will pay too much for them when we're excited and when we sell things, we will sell them for too little when we are in fear. When your emotions are running high, your intelligence is low; they are inversely proportional to each other. I will give you some advice on how plastic surgery will save you thousands of pounds....... get your credit card and cut it to pieces. I have devised a couple of hints to prevent me from falling for the instant gratification trap:

I use cash for any purchases I make. There is something more real about paying with cash; you can see it leave your hands. It has made me think twice about whether I really need to spend when I see the cash about to leave my hands.

When I am about to purchase anything I look at the amount and times it by four. For example, if I am about to buy a cappuccino for £5, I will tell myself it is really costing me £20. In most businesses, your profit is 50% of turnover and you have 50% tax to pay on this profit. So for every £20 I turn over in business, I get £10 in profit (50% expenses, or 50% associate fees) and out of that £10 I pay tax on 50%, leaving me with £5. So now can you see why that £5 purchase really cost me £20? It works really well when you are deciding to buy any new dental equipment.

Contrast principle: – this is a real killer and I have fallen for this trap many times. Let's say you have two items on your shopping list: some socks and a new suit. You go into a shop and find a nice pair of socks for £15. You are about to pay for them but recall that the same pair of socks are on sale for £8 at another store fifteen minutes away. What would you do? Most people would make the trip to save the £7. Now you go and look for your suit. You find one for £855 and decide to buy it. As you're waiting to pay, the customer behind you whispers to you that the exact same suit is on sale at £848 at another store, fifteen minutes away. Do you make this trip? Most people would not. But wait: isn't it the same £7 in each case? We make our decisions in a relative way and compare them locally to the available alternative! I used this to my advantage in dentistry. Whenever a patient was undergoing an extensive treatment I would ask if they wanted teeth whitening too at £397. Now £397 compared to a £10,000 treatment plan is not that much, but that same patient may possibly baulk at paying £397 if they were only considering teeth whitening. Before any GDC committee members write to me, I would only offer services that would enhance and benefit the patient.

<u>C – Compounding</u> – This occurs when you invest money and allow it to continuously reinvest itself, such as holding property for the long term. Let's say you deiced to have a game of 18 hole golf and you bet just 10p on the first hole and then doubled your bet every hole thereafter. The last hole would be worth £13,107.20. No matter how little you start with, you must start now. Saving £150 a month (that's £5 a day – a large JD and coke) at a 15% annual return for 30 years yields £1,051,000. Warren Buffett, one of the richest men in the world, understood the importance of

compounding: *'I just can't bring myself to buy a new car because if I spend that amount of money it's going to cost me millions in the future.'*

Here are some tips and strategies I have learnt and use to make sure I win the money game:

Reset your money blueprint – throw away your old negative beliefs about money and wealth and change them to the belief that you can do great things if you become wealthy and by adding more value you will attract more money.

Don't be a money victim – life does not happen to you, you create your life. What you focus on expands; don't focus on problems but solutions. Try this exercise for the next seven days – do not complain about anything. This is hard and when I did this the first few times I only lasted hours. Then I stretched it to a day and eventually got to seven days and now I very rarely complain.

- Money only makes you more of what you are already. Making more money won't change you experience of life. Nothing has meaning, apart from the meaning you give it.

- Take action and be 100% committed. The more you learn, the more you earn.

- One last surefire way to double your money is to fold it once and put it back in your pocket!

Winning the money game.

Mistakes

1. There are different skills required to make money than keep money. Become a specialist to make the money initially, like becoming a dentist, and then consider multiple streams of income to keep your wealth, such as property.

2. If you can't handle what you have right now, you won't receive any more. I was once out with my kids in the park and as all normal kids do when they heard the music of the ice cream van they jumped with excitement. Being a soft touch I agreed to get them each an ice cream. They both opted for the 99p whipped flake ice cream. (By the way, I don't know why they call it a "ninety nine" as it's never that price!) As they were walking back they both dropped their ice creams. I gave it a few seconds and then the tears started appearing. What does a dad do? He doesn't want to see the kids upset – so we went back to the ice cream van. However, the kids spotted a triple scoop ice cream and now they want that one...What would you do? Buy the triple scoop or stick to the 99p flake with single scoop? If you said get the triple scoop...no...if they couldn't handle the single scoop, how will they possibly handle the triple scoop? It's setting them up for failure. This is similar to what happens to a lot of lottery winners who, after a few years, end up in the same financial situation they were before they won the lottery. When it comes to money, you get what you truly intend to get.

I have made the following error when managing my finances and I see a lot of newly qualified dentists committing the same mistake. You can either create the lifestyle or wealth, but not both at the beginning. You can't build up wealth in the long term if you're a flash Harry (no pun intended) right now when you have not created the wealth. No need to have expensive cars or live in a penthouse when you have just started your journey to financial freedom. Buy appreciating assets and then you can use the income from these assets to buy your cars.

Action plan

Spend a few minutes answering these three questions. What are your reasons to make money:

- Lifestyle – what are your reasons? What will it give you?

- Contribution to other people's lifestyles – higher purpose, family, charity – imagine a stadium full of 75,000 people, then imagine that amount of people die every day from starvation

- Personal and professional development

Summary

There is nothing wrong in wanting to get rich. The desire for riches is really the desire for a richer, fuller and more abundant life.

Winning the money game.

Once you understand the psychology of money you can now look at how you can make money work for you instead of working for your money, which we will cover in the next chapter.

Financial Freedom Formula Allows You to Never Work Again ⋯ Unless You Choose To

Once you understand the psychology of money from the previous chapter you can now look at how you can make money work for you instead of working for money.

'The rich invest their money and spend what is left, the poor spend their money and invest what is left.' Jim Rohn

If as a dentist you want to go from trading time for money to never working again......unless you choose to – read on.

Did you know that the average person only has two months of savings before they run out of money? It's not what you're doing now that makes you money, it's what you are not doing.

Becoming wealthy is a game and you need to know the rules of the game to play and have any chance of winning. Who would have thought there was a hooker in rugby? Maybe that's where Tiger Woods got confused. In his book 'Delivering Happiness' Tony Hsieh writes, "Don't play games that you don't understand, even if you see lots of other people making money from them."

Rich vs Wealthy

Who wants to be rich?...Who wants to be wealthy?...Who wants to be both?....What's the difference? The first difference relates to a financial sense. Rich people only have the money. Whilst wealthy people also have the money, they know how to make it too. For example, someone could be rich from winning the lottery, a large inheritance, a high paying job such as a city banker or even a dentist. If they don't understand how to be wealthy, then there is a real risk that they will lose all their riches or these riches will disappear once they stop working.

Being wealthy is defined as that status of an individual's existing financial resources that supports his or her way of living for a longer duration, even if he or she does not work to generate a recurring income. Wealthy people can build sustainable wealth that can last for years through asset investments producing multiple streams of income. Or another way to look at it is what we have organised to take care of how many lives for how many forward days. In summary, the difference is financial knowledge. If you notice, there are a lot of so-called 'get-rich-quick' schemes but there are no 'get-wealthy-quick' schemes.

The second classification or difference is what you have contributed to society. This is why I felt so privileged to be in dentistry. We have the potential to transform and enhance so many patients' lives – that is true wealth in my eyes. Rich just means having money. There are many rich people out there but not many of them are truly wealthy by definition. Wealthy people are not just rich in the pocket, but in the mind as well. They are the innovators and world-changers who have a significant impact on the lives of a great number of people.

Wealth means completely different things to different people. Mother Teresa's definition of wealth is probably a little different to Bill Gates', and again probably a little different from yours or mine.

Wealthy inside and out. This story appeared in the March 2013 issue of Success Magazine. The editor was having lunch with a school friend (Andy) who was an engineer; he was married to a school teacher and had three children. They had modest incomes, lived in a nice house and had family holidays. He coached the local kids' football team and they were happy. Another old school friend (Jake) rushed past them, got into his Aston Martin and drove off. Andy commented, "Imagine being that guy." You could understand Andy's admiration at Jake's car, penthouse flat, private jet. However, behind the scenes, Jake was going through a messy divorce. He was also under extreme stress to deliver at his work, so he drank too much, led an unhealthy lifestyle and was too busy to see his children. One can have lots of money but still be poor. Financially, yes Jake was miles better off, but emotionally, Andy was the real winner. Wealth is not a state of bank account, it's a state of mind.

There are actually seven types of wealth and you'll notice this will relate to the wheel of life I introduced you to in chapter one.

- Physical wealth – having the optimal health and energy in your body that makes everything you do possible

- Emotional wealth – where you live emotionally is the quality of your life, a great sense of meaning

- The wealth of relationships – who loves you? who do you love? how do you treat each other?

- The wealth of time – are you really enjoying what you are doing? Does time seems to disappear in a good way?

- The wealth of work/career/mission –

- Financial wealth – see rest of chapter

- The wealth of contributing and celebration – progress and happiness comes from growing and giving, getting outside of yourself by adding value to other people's lives. Contribution completes the feeling of being truly alive, but you also have to celebrate life's successes, victories, and all the things to be grateful for. (I think I have mastered that aspect – any excuse for a drink or party!)

Financial Security vs Financial Independence vs Financial Freedom

Financial security – The amount of money that covers food, housing, cars, travel and basic entertainment – that's good, at least the Jack Daniels is covered.

Financial independence – To have accumulated an amount of money so large that you are no longer influenced or controlled by others to sustain a "comfortable" lifestyle. This is where you don't have to work and you have broken free of the shackles of trading time for money.

Financial freedom – The ability to live the lifestyle you desire (everything you can possibly think of) without having to work or rely on anyone else for money.

Level 1 – Financial Security – enough passive income to cover your bare essentials such as food, shelter, utility bills, essential expenses such as clothing, insurance, motor maintenance etc. For most people this figure would be less that £2,000pcm.

Level 2 – Financial Independence – enough passive income to maintain your current lifestyle. For most people this would be between £2,000pcm-£5,000pcm.

Level 3 – Financial Freedom – enough passive income to live your dream lifestyle. For most people this would be +£10,000pcm.

Now we know what we are aiming for. Before we look at how we are going to achieve each stepping stone, we need to analyse exactly where we are. This exercise is vital. If you don't do this preparation first, then it would be similar to playing a game of darts blindfolded. You would be using the 'pin the tail on the donkey approach' to achieve wealth creation.

Draw four columns on a piece of a paper. In the first column write the three levels of finance you want to achieve – Security, Independence, Freedom. In the second column write how much money you would need to obtain to reach each of the three levels. In the third column write how much passive income you have coming in at the moment. Work out the difference between the figures in the second and third columns for each level, and write this amount in the final column. This is the target passive income figure you need to work towards.

Why not get a pen and paper and work out what figures you would need to achieve each definition? Then you can work backwards on how you are going to achieve that passive income. To keep this nice and simple, Financial Security equals a basic essential lifestyle, Financial Independence equals a comfortable lifestyle and Financial Freedom equals your dream or ideal lifestyle. Therefore, once you have Financial Security covered, Financial Independence is a stepping stone towards Financial Freedom.

What does financial freedom mean to you? Does it mean freedom from having to work, yet still being able to enjoy life without uncertainty about money? Does it mean having your life's basic costs covered? Having more time to do the things you really want to do? For me it's dropping the kids off to school in the morning and strolling back to car whilst all the other parents are running around like headless chickens trying not to be late for the rat race.

Stop trading time for money.

How to achieve financial freedom

This is brought to you in the form of – P.I.S.S.

There is a science of getting rich, and it's an exact science. There are certain laws that govern the process of acquiring riches. Once these laws are learnt and mastered, anyone can get rich with mathematical certainty.

P.I.S.S. = Passive income + investment income + savings + simplify

<u>Passive income</u> – As we know, passive income is income derived from you not working directly to generate it. It does not mean you won't initially need to put some work in, but it is the 'set and forget' strategy, where once you set it up, on the whole you can forget about it. The best type of passive income is property. Not only do you have someone (tenant) paying your debt (mortgage) you also have surplus income (rent) coming in monthly and over the long term you are holding onto an appreciating asset.

<u>Investment income</u> – This is derived from the capital gains you make when selling property, dividends from shares, etc. I, like the next person, want to enjoy my life now, so passive income is good, but you can't enjoy its benefits immediately when you are starting out. Therefore I always advocate selling a few properties instead of keeping them all, so you can get the money out and either reinvest it or enjoy it.

<u>Savings</u> – Always have some money stashed away in a long term savings account for any emergencies or that deal of a lifetime where you need to move fast.

<u>Simplify</u> – When you are starting out on the road to wealth creation, you need to cut down any unnecessary expenses and invest as much money as possible early on. With the power of

compounding, small regular contributions early on are much better than big lump contributions in later life. Do not live beyond your means. You can do that later when you have reached financial independence.

Or to simplify the above:

Passive income – income without work, ongoing passive business income (business working for you), e.g. property portfolio

Investment income – (money working for you) – doing a joint venture with me on property deals

Savings – liquid cash that can easily be accessed for emergencies or that great deal

Simplify – spend less than what you earn and invest the difference. Cut your coat according to your cloth.

Five tips

Use debit and not credit cards

Slim your wallet down –have just one credit card for emergencies only

Do not shop online

Bank online

Visit cash machine once a week only

Have a primary source of income that covers your expenses

and then build up your passive income in the background until you don't need your primary income. That's what I did; I did not give up dentistry until I had a well established, proven source of passive income. You don't want to be naked and alone. No man can serve two masters – concentrate on one and build up the other in the background.

Multiple streams of income – Many people assume this means different types of investments or business opportunities. However, any new venture has a steep learning curve that takes time and energy. My definition of multiple streams of income is different revenue streams from the same business. For example, with property I have numerous income streams such as:

- buying and holding properties

- buying and selling properties

- selling deals to investors

- property training via seminars

- leaflet distribution

- call handling

- deal closing

- referral fees from strategic alliances

- rent to rent

- products – books/DVDs
- lease options
- forums/membership sites
- bridging finance
- meet the surveyor
- Utility Warehouse
- tenant referencing
- title splitting
- commercial property
- hostels
- guaranteed rent
- planning gains

Multiple streams of income are for staying rich, but not getting rich. The top 10% of the Sunday Times Rich List are specialists and not generalists. They made their money initially on one sector by focusing on it and mastering it. Once that business was either sold or running without them they looked at other forms of passive income. When looking at multiple streams of income I follow the CYA rule – Cover Your Arse. Evaluate all consequences upfront.

Stop trading time for money.

Harry's humour corner

Lottery is a tax on people who are bad at maths.

You can make money from absolutely anything. Twenty years ago if you came up with the idea of selling bottled water, they would have sent you to the funny farm. By the way, did you know Evian spelt backwards is naïve?

I would like to be so rich that when I write a cheque, the bank bounces.

Benjamin Franklin may have discovered electricity, but it was the man who invented the meter who made the money.

Trouble is even if you win the rat race, you are still a rat.

A rich dentist, a poor dentist and the tooth fairy were walking down the road together. They walked past an ATM machine and noticed £50 on the floor. There was nobody else around, so one of them decided to take the money. Who took it??? The rich dentist.............the other two don't exist.

I saw the book 'The Millionaire Next Door', at Waterstones and went to the assistant and asked her if I bought two copies, would I become a double millionaire!

Quotes

'Be your own best financial advisor, invest in products you understand with people you trust.' – Donald Trump

'Without a financial education, it takes a lot more money to get rich

and a lot more money to stay rich. The higher your financial IQ, the less money it takes you to get rich.' – Robert Kiyosaki

'There are two rules to investing. Rule one is never lose money. Rule two is see rule 1 .' – Warren Buffett.

Summary

Stop trading time for money. Only a few weeks ago I was on a train with two employees of the train company. They had just been paid and were discussing their pay slips. For over an hour they were arguing and debating why one had a £7 deduction taken out. I could not believe it. They should have invested that 60 minutes in financial education and learning about passive income.

What can I do to become more wealthy? Learn from those who have already proved the path to wealth creation. Learn from those that have generated the ideas, laid out the vision, assembled a plan and fought the adversaries that lay ahead of any great success story.

Wealth Through Property

In my final chapter I will share with you my weapon of choice used by over 80% of The Sunday Times Rich List to become wealthy and achieve financial freedom: the asset of the rich..........property.

Despite the recent economic downturn, property investment is as popular and rewarding as it ever has been, as long as you know what you are doing[1]. This asset of the rich[2] creates enormous wealth for many thousands of people that allows them to work when they want to and achieve financial freedom.

Whilst talking to my dental colleagues about property, I was disheartened that many were either putting off wealth creation via property because of incorrect information or were investing in property, but not in the most profitable way.

When I first started investing in property back in 2002, I made the same mistakes that many of my dental colleagues are making. I then learnt over time, with guidance, and gained the necessary experience to understand and make use of the professional property game. This is where professional, sophisticated investors use strategies that allow them to benefit from sustainable cash flow whilst building long term assets for the future. I learnt from these mentors, took action and implemented their strategies and I have built a property portfolio worth over £7 million.

Has the recent property crash changed your expectations and

turned your attitudes on their head? As Warren Buffett stated, '*Be fearful when everyone is greedy and be greedy when everyone else is fearful.*' There has never been a better time to invest in property and secure your future. The best time is now.

'*Study of economics usually reveals that the best time to buy anything is last year.*' – Marty Allen.

Many experts are labeling property as the new pension for the wealthy. Right now, today we have the following factors making property attractive:

- we have price retractions
- we have the home buyers scheme
- we have the government's home buyers scheme
- We have a net increase in population in the UK
- We have record low interest rates

Property is a vehicle for having sustainable cash flow whilst building long term assets for the future. Profit from Property.

The benefits of investing in property are numerous

Leverage – you can leverage bank loans secured on the property (known as mortgages) and benefit from 100% of the gain. You would normally put down a deposit of around 25% and the remaining 75% would be covered via the mortgage – unlike other investments such as shares, where you would need to put in 100% of the whole amount. For example, a property is bought for £100,000. You would put in 25% = £25,000 and the mortgage lender the remaining 75% = £75,000. Let's say in ten years the property is now worth £200,000. You get to keep this £100,000 gain and your original investment was only £25,000k (25%).

Set and forget, work once and get paid forever. Once you have found the property and tenant, then you will need minimal time to manage the property (outsource to letting agent).

As a dentist, would you be interested in going from 0 to 27 properties in 24 months or £0 to £8,000 passive income per month or from £0 to £7m+ property portfolio? If you would, then you will need to implement the strategies I personally use to make a killing in the property market. It's the strategies of the professional property game to build a multi million pound portfolio that will take care of you and your family for years to come.

Income or Growth

What are your wealth creation goals? As I mentioned in chapter one, you need to know your goals in terms of where you want to go. In chapter five we looked at the amount of money you will need to achieve financial independence. You will initially need to decide whether you want income or growth from your property investing. Do you intend to keep the property for income (holding for long term and making rental profits – known as BTL – Buy To Let) or are you planning to dispose of the property to benefit from the realisation of capital (known as BTS – Buy To Sell, or flipping), and if so, in what timescale?

Directly – If you have the time, passion and knowledge then there is no reason why you can't do it yourself. I do. Like you, I started with zero knowledge and over a decade learnt the strategies and built the power team to help me succeed. You can compress decades into days by attending one of my seminars where I teach the strategies I personally use in today's property market. If you invest in yourself then there are normally two strategies you will use:

(i) – Building a portfolio – keeping the property for long term to let and realise the capital growth in the future, maybe as a pension pot.

(ii) – Buy to sell – making income from property either to replace or supplement your dental income.

Indirectly – you may not have the time or passion to learn the rules of the professional property game, but still want to use property as a vehicle to achieve your financial freedom and this can be achieved.

Joint venture – you can partner up with someone who has the experience and capability of finding bargain properties (like me) and supply the cash and both of you will profit from the deals. I have done numerous joint venture deals and as long as the ground rules are laid out on the table, it all goes well.

Purchase deals – you don't have to source the properties

yourself. Instead you pay a relatively small fee for someone to find you the deals and either keep the property to rent or sell on for immediate profit.

Profit from Property.

Rules of the professional property game

You make your money when you buy and not when you sell. This is critical for your success in building a property portfolio.

How do we find these bargain properties?

This process comes to you in the form of the BAD AV – Buy At Discount or Add Value.

Be a problem solver. The more and bigger problems you can solve, the more money you will make.

BAD – Buy At Discount

Look at the seller's circumstances and not the property itself. Person before property. Find the reason why they are selling, their motivation.

As mentioned previously we need to look at the reason why someone is selling their house compared to the house itself. We need them to have motivation; the speed and certainty of the sale is more critical than the final selling price. There are many reasons why someone may be motivated to sell quickly, such as:

- Financial difficulties – If you think nobody cares about you, try missing a couple of mortgage payments

- Marriage split

- Relocation

- Inherited property

- Stuck in chain for a long time

- Found their ideal next home

- Property is unmodernised

Case example – Property value – £250,000; Purchase price – £180,000; Selling price – £235,000; Profit in 3 months £55,000. The seller responded to one of my marketing strategies. He was emigrating and had a very tight timeframe. He could not afford to waste time with estate agents and endless viewings and no guarantee of a sale. He was happy to clear his mortgage of £145,000. However I said I could clear his mortgage and leave him with an extra £35,000 for moving costs and rent for his new home abroad. He was delighted with this deal. We wrapped it all up in under a month and he had all the loose ends tied up before he made a fresh start abroad. Win-win for both of us.

Ethics

We are problem solvers. Firstly you need to be sure you are prompt, professional and courteous with all your dealings with a motivated seller so they are confident you can deliver your promise. Just as we do an initial consultation with our dental patients, you need to listen to them, explain to them that everything is confidential and then offer them various solutions (treatment plans) with the appropriate benefits and risks associated with each one. As a dentist this comes naturally to us and I think we have this as a benefit compared to other property investors. On the other hand, we are also not a charity and we do need to make money and all the sellers I have visited understand this when I have explained it to them. In summary, you should always go in with the attitude of "How can I help this seller with their situation?"

I turn away more deals away than I take. I can and do refer some to estate agents, if they are not desperate to sell and can wait. I always advise that the best price they will get is from an estate agent at near full market value. I know the best estate agents in my town and if they have a crap agent that is not proactive, I recommend them to change once their contract has ended. I give them low cost or free tips on how to dress the property. I always say my offer and solution should be their last resort.

When you do find a deal, do what you promised. Don't mess the seller around, as they are already under enough stress with their situation. Communicate regularly – at least once a week – with the seller and with the solicitors. Believe in the win-win deal and you will be able to sleep at night.

Case example – I visited a house where the young couple were very distressed. The wife had inherited the property from her parents, who sadly had passed away. Initially they were mortgage free, but they needed an urgent loan and borrowed £15,000, using the £165,000 house as security. They fell behind on their loan payments and the loan company decided to repossess the house for the £15,000. They were on the verge of losing this house, being kicked out and having no money until the loan and all associated charges had been paid off. They even told me to just clear the £15,000 and have the house; they just wanted the problem to go away. I could have bought a house worth £165,000 for £15,000, but I believed in a win-win situation. So I said I would buy it at £132,000. That would give me plenty of equity, which I was happy with, and they could clear the loan of £15,000 and associated costs and still be left with over £100,000 in their bank account to start afresh.

AV – Add Value

The second strategy is to find a property that needs work doing to it that looks a bit tired. The work can range from minor cosmetic works such as new kitchen, bathrooms, lick of paint and new carpets to fixing major structural defects. This is where you need to know your numbers before you make an offer. You first work out the costs of the works required to the house and the final realistic selling price, then you calculate how much profit you want to make. Add the selling costs and then base your offer on these figures.

I am often asked the following questions regarding my profit from property strategies:

"It sounds too good to be true – if it does work why are you sharing the rules of the professional property game with us?"

The answer is two-fold. Firstly, I work in a very small area and I leave the rest of the UK to other investors. It's very unlikely that you will be marketing the same area as me. Secondly, I need your money. Due to my large portfolio I have reached the threshold of how many properties I can have with each bank, so they won't lend me any more money against further property purchases. It doesn't make sense to me, but that's banking logic for you. The definition of bank is someone that gives you an umbrella when it's sunny, but the moment it rains, it wants it back. Also I believe in the power of leverage.

'I'd rather have 1% of the efforts of 100 people than 100% of my own efforts.' – Jean Paul Getty.

"I have no or little money."

There are ways we can help you raise finance. You can, like me, use other people's money and joint venture with them. Also, there is another strategy which I teach where you can control a house for £1.

Actions to do immediately

If you intend to invest directly in property, make sure you have solid foundations before you start generating any leads:

Credit score – check to make sure mortgage companies will lend to you. I use www.experian.co.uk.

Power team – find your mortgage brokers, solicitors, estate agents, leaflet distributors, insurance brokers, letting agents, gas safety checkers, bridgers, tradespeople, surveyors, other investors, mentors

Funds available – what funds can you easily access to help you finance any deals that may present themselves to you?

Let's say you have inherited a million pounds but it is in a box on top of a mountain. You have to climb this mountain personally to get this money and you only have one year to get it and then it's gone. What would you need?.........A mentor, training programme, discipline....basically the same as you would need if you wanted to create wealth.

'While I was stupidly messing around with the Football Association, others were making a killing in property. It was a waste of my time and talent.' – Lord Sugar

Five biggest mistakes made by property investors

Whilst I have been investing in property for over ten years, I see time and time again the same mistakes investors make when they start their property journey.

Mistake 1 – Location

Solution

Investors look at a location that is not within travelling distance to where they live. I would advise you to invest in an area that is no more than 40 minutes drive for you. The advantages of investing in a location near you are that you will know the area and it is easily accessible for you. Novice investors get swayed by locations further afield, especially as the further up north you go the rental yields are better. But unless you have someone trusted that can manage the property, I would steer away from this.

Mistake 2 – Not treating it as a business

Solution

Just like your dental/medical business, property is exactly the same. You need to work out your business plan and goals. Factor in how much capital you have and what your cashflow requirements are. What contingency plans do you have? When will you exit the business? Don't treat property investing as a hobby, because if you do, it will become a very expensive hobby.

Mistake 3 – Not buying from motivated sellers

Solution

You make your money when you buy. You are more interested in the reason why the person is selling the property and to a lesser extent, the property itself. 99% of sellers will not be motivated and will want full asking price for their properties. You do not want to waste your time and energy on these deals. Look at the reason why they are selling and then you can negotiate a much better buying price for their property.

Mistake 4 – Buying only for capital appreciation

Solution

I have personally made this mistake myself. I brought some properties in London but the rent was not covering the mortgage and I had to put money in every month. At that time I did not mind as I knew long term the price would go up. Wrong. Yes, capital appreciation is good, but treat it like a bonus. As I mentioned in mistake #2, treat your property investing as a business. You want positive cashflow from day one and every month thereafter; you do not want to be putting your hard-earned cash into any property investing. Therefore look for high yielding rental properties. In the south of England this normally means renting room by room; in the north you can often rent to a single let (family) and still have good positive cashflow per month.

Mistake 5 – Buying overseas or new builds

Solution

This is more of an ego boost. You want this on your asset column: property in Dubai, Florida, Spain, etc. This comes back to the problem that you are trusting someone else to manage your property. What happens if something goes wrong with the property? You can't just hop on a plane and double check it; you have to rely on the overseas agent.

Also stay away from new builds. They may be all new and modern but with your business hat on look at the figures realistically. The problem will be when you come to rent out the properties. All these shiny new apartments will come onto the rental market at the same time. What do you think your potential tenant will do? It is all about supply and demand – your new build will just become a commodity and the problem with this is the cheapest price will win. So all the landlords will start dropping their rent until they eventually find tenants. Then you have some developers trying to overcome this problem by having a rent guarantee for one or two years. This is all good, but you are only delaying the problem; the rents will drop dramatically once the guarantee period is over.

Summary

My five step process for property success is MRBLT.

Motivation – Only work with motivated sellers.

Rental demand strong – Choose your location and type of property carefully so you can easily rent it.

Buffer – Have spare cash that is easily accessible for unexpected repairs or if the deal of a lifetime comes along.

Long term and hold – Keep some properties and hold them for capital appreciation; remember the law of compounding.

Time – The time is now – TNT – Today Not Tomorrow.

10 Tips to Escape the Rat Race

'The trouble with being in the rat race is that even if you win, you're still a rat.' – Lily Tomlin

In this chapter I will outline 10 tips you can do immediately to stop working for money and let money work for you.

These tips follow the acronym **MAGSTRIPES**, which is ironic as these occur on the back of credit cards, which is probably the number one reason why most people are stuck in the rat race and never achieve financial freedom.

M – Mindset

We live in two worlds: our inner world and our outer world. This inner world (thoughts, emotions, beliefs) controls our outer world (external events). However, most people live the opposite way – their outer world controls their inner world.

Without a vision or belief that you can escape the rat race, you never will as your inner world reflects your outer world. You must believe.

A – Automation

I believe in the set and forget process. Set up the systems and processes and then you can forget about it. You only have a limited amount of resources, so why not automate and leverage this to your advantage? Leverage comes in many forms, such as other people's money, other people's time, other people's contacts, other people's experiences.

My mistake was that I was doing everything myself and also thinking no one could do it better than me. I was working all the hours and getting nowhere. Once I leveraged and automated everything I could, the earth did not collapse. In fact my productivity increased the less I did myself.

G – Goals

This relates to point #1. You need to have your goals well planned and thought out before you can experience any of the results you want.

Stop reading now and plan your one year goals in the following categories:

- Health and wellbeing
- Wealth
- Friends and family
- Playtime
- Relationships and romance
- Career/job
- Personal space/personal development
- Contribution/spirituality

Then break them down into three month, one month and weekly goals. For example, if I wanted to lose 12kg during the year my three month goal would be to lose 4kg, the monthly goal 1kg and the weekly goal 1/4kg.

S – Save

I have this jar at home and every month without fail I will put 10% of my income (post tax) in it. Obviously I put the cash in the savings account, but I put a piece of paper into the jar to illustrate the amount I have put in that month. This is never to be touched. It is my safety net, so that I will always have some savings available no matter what.

T – Time

Are you in BUSiness or are you just BUSYness. Forget a 'to do' list; have a results based list. You can save yourself a lot of time by firstly following point #2 about automation. Then when you are left with the tasks you need to do, the first question you need to ask yourself is, 'What result/outcome do I want from this?' This will save you a lot of time on unproductive tasks.

R – Rewards

I love this bit. Constantly reward yourself when you are moving closer to any goals. Constant and repetitive rewards will motivate you to continue. It may be as simple as going to your favourite restaurant or having a bottle of champagne.

I – Invest

Learn about different forms of investment by reading books and attending seminars. Pick a couple you understand and start as soon as you can. The power of compounding will mean your initial small investment will grow to a large pot.

'Compound interest is the eighth wonder of the world. He who understands it, earns it ... he who doesn't ... pays it.' – Albert Einstein

P – Passive Income

This is an income received on a regular basis, with little effort required to maintain it. It is the number one reason why the rich get richer. They, like all of us, are limited with time and hourly rate on how much they can earn themselves. In my opinion the best form of passive income is derived from property. You have an appreciating asset whose liabilities (mortgage payments) are paid by someone else (the tenant) and you have surplus rental income left over every month (passive income). That's why over 80% of the Sunday Times Rich List made their money either directly or indirectly from property.

E – Education

When you decided to become a dentist, did you read a few books, attend weekend seminars and then start practising immediately? No. You spent a committed amount of time continuously over a period of time. So why not do the same when considering your financial future. There is an old saying, *'Formal education will make you a living, but self education will make you a fortune.'*

S – Simplify

Don't live beyond your means. You don't have to spend everything you earn. When you are first starting out creating wealth you can either live the high life or invest your money; you can't do both. I use the jar system, where in addition to 10% of my post tax income going into the savings jar, I have 10% that is allocated to my investment jar, without fail, every month.

Visit www.dentalpropertyclub.co.uk and download this report for FREE "10 Secrets To Successful Property Investing For Busy Dentists"

Conclusion

'People who have achieved great success are not necessarily more skillful or intelligent than others. What separates them is their burning desire and thirst for knowledge. The more one knows, the more one achieves.' – Robin Sharma

If you recall at the beginning I mentioned that all the pieces will come together as long as you follow the recipe. The journey has not ended; it has just begun. Be clear on your goals, manage your time well, control your mind, understand your beliefs about money, create your own financial freedom formula and use property as a vehicle to stop trading time for money.

The Dental Property Club can help you achieve your financial goals quicker and easier. You can learn from my 10 years plus experience in property, take away my strategies and invest in property directly yourself or we can partner up using your cash and my time and experience to profit jointly from my property deals. The ball is in your court now, but whatever you decide follow the E.D.A. model: Education – Decision – Action.

'Do not follow where the path lies, go instead where there is no path and leave a trail.'